GRATITUI
JOURNAL
GOLD

This Journal belongs to

_____

Copyright © 2019 Brenda Nathan
All rights reserved.

ISBN: 9781089505730

Gratitude

Gratitude is a feeling of appreciation for what one has. It is a feeling of thankfulness for the blessings we have received. Feeling gratitude in the present moment makes you happier and more relaxed, and improves your overall health and well-being.

Affirmations are words that we consciously choose to say. When we repeat affirmations, they get imprinted in the subconscious mind. Therefore, it is key that we use positive affirmations if we want to create a positive life for ourselves.

There is an exercise at the beginning of this journal to complete before starting your daily record of gratitude and affirmation.

By keeping a record of your gratitude in a journal, you will store positive energy, gain clarity in your life, and have greater control of your thoughts and emotions.

Each day, write down three to five things that you are grateful for in this journal and turn your ordinary moments into blessings.

A gentle word, a kind look, a good-natured smile can work wonders and accomplish miracles. ~ *William Hazlitt*

People I am *Grateful* for:

_____
_____
_____
_____
_____
_____
_____

Top 10 memorable events in my life that I am *Grateful* for:

1. _____
2. _____
3. _____
4. _____
5. _____
6. _____
7. _____
8. _____
9. _____
10. _____

People I have made a difference to and am *Grateful* for having had this opportunity:

_____
_____
_____
_____
_____
_____

Top 10 places I have visited and am *Grateful* for:

1. _____
2. _____
3. _____
4. _____
5. _____
6. _____
7. _____
8. _____
9. _____
10. _____

The times when I have laughed so hard that I cried and which I am now *Grateful* for:

Top 10 things that I was scared to do but am now *Grateful* for having done:

1.
2.
3.
4.
5.
6.
7.
8.
9.
10.

Things I have now which I am *Grateful* for:

Top 10 teachable moments from my past that I am now *Grateful* for:

1.
2.
3.
4.
5.
6.
7.
8.
9.
10.

Something that I am looking forward to:
_____
_____
_____
_____
_____
_____

Top 10 things I'd like to accomplish:
1. _____
2. _____
3. _____
4. _____
5. _____
6. _____
7. _____
8. _____
9. _____
10. _____

Day: _____ *Date:* ____ / ____ / ____

Today I am *Grateful* for _____

_____

_____

_____

_____

Today's Affirmation _____

Courtesies of a small and trivial character are the ones which strike deepest in the grateful and appreciating heart. ~ *Henry Clay*

Day: _____ *Date:* ____ / ____ / ____

Today I am *Grateful* for _____

_____

_____

_____

_____

Today's Affirmation _____

Day: _____ *Date:* ___/___/___

Today I am *Grateful* for _____

_____
_____
_____
_____
_____

Today's Affirmation _____

> Being deeply loved by someone gives you strength, while loving someone deeply gives you courage. ~ *Lao Tzu*

Day: _____ *Date:* ___/___/___

Today I am *Grateful* for _____

_____
_____
_____
_____
_____

Today's Affirmation _____

Day: _____ Date: ____/____/____

Today I am *Grateful* for _____

_____

_____

_____

_____

Today's Affirmation _____

The most certain sign of wisdom is cheerfulness. ~ Michel de Montaigne

Day: _____ Date: ____/____/____

Today I am *Grateful* for _____

_____

_____

_____

_____

Today's Affirmation _____

Day: _____ Date: ____/____/____

Today I am *Grateful* for _____

_____
_____
_____
_____

Today's Affirmation _____

> Keep love in your heart. A life without it is like a sunless garden when the flowers are dead. ~ *Oscar Wilde*

Day: _____ Date: ____/____/____

Today I am *Grateful* for _____

_____
_____
_____
_____

Today's Affirmation _____

Day: _____ *Date:* ____/____/____

Today I am *Grateful* for _____

_____
_____
_____
_____

Today's Affirmation _____

> Let us be grateful to people who make us happy, they are the charming gardeners who make our souls blossom. ~ *Marcel Proust*

Day: _____ *Date:* ____/____/____

Today I am *Grateful* for _____

_____
_____
_____
_____

Today's Affirmation _____

Day: _____ Date: ____/____/____

Today I am *Grateful* for _____

_____
_____
_____
_____

Today's Affirmation _____

The thankful receiver bears a plentiful harvest. ~ *William Blake*

Day: _____ Date: ____/____/____

Today I am *Grateful* for _____

_____
_____
_____
_____

Today's Affirmation _____

Day: _____ *Date:* ____/____/____

Today I am *Grateful* for _____

_____

_____

_____

_____

Today's Affirmation _____

Our greatest glory is not in never falling, but in rising every time we fall.
~ *Confucius*

Day: _____ *Date:* ____/____/____

Today I am *Grateful* for _____

_____

_____

_____

_____

Today's Affirmation _____

Day: _____ Date: ____/____/____

Today I am *Grateful* for _____

_____
_____
_____
_____

Today's Affirmation _____

Happiness is not an ideal of reason, but of imagination. ~ *Immanuel Kant*

Day: _____ Date: ____/____/____

Today I am *Grateful* for _____

_____
_____
_____
_____

Today's Affirmation _____

Day: _____ Date: ____/____/____

Today I am *Grateful* for _____

_____

_____

_____

_____

Today's Affirmation _____

The art of being happy lies in the power of extracting happiness from common things. ~ Henry Ward Beecher

Day: _____ Date: ____/____/____

Today I am *Grateful* for _____

_____

_____

_____

_____

Today's Affirmation _____

Day: _____ Date: ___/___/___

Today I am *Grateful* for _____

_____
_____
_____
_____

Today's Affirmation _____

> The clearest way into the Universe is through a forest wilderness.
> ~ *John Muir*

Day: _____ Date: ___/___/___

Today I am *Grateful* for _____

_____
_____
_____
_____

Today's Affirmation _____

Day: _____ *Date:* ____/____/____

Today I am *Grateful* for _____

_____
_____
_____
_____
_____

Today's Affirmation _____

Gratitude is a state of being and should be directed towards everything that you are creating in this life.

Day: _____ *Date:* ____/____/____

Today I am *Grateful* for _____

_____
_____
_____
_____
_____

Today's Affirmation _____

Day: _____ Date: ___/___/___

Today I am *Grateful* for _____

_____
_____
_____
_____

Today's Affirmation _____

> The pleasure which we most rarely experience gives us greatest delight.
> ~ *Epictetus*

Day: _____ Date: ___/___/___

Today I am *Grateful* for _____

_____
_____
_____
_____

Today's Affirmation _____

Day: _____ *Date:* ____/____/____

Today I am *Grateful* for _____

_____

_____

_____

_____

Today's Affirmation _____

> Our happiness depends on wisdom all the way. ~ *Sophocles*

Day: _____ *Date:* ____/____/____

Today I am *Grateful* for _____

_____

_____

_____

_____

Today's Affirmation _____

Day: _____ Date: ___/___/___

Today I am *Grateful* for _____

_____
_____
_____
_____

Today's Affirmation _____

To live is so startling it leaves little time for anything else.
~ Emily Dickinson

Day: _____ Date: ___/___/___

Today I am *Grateful* for _____

_____
_____
_____
_____

Today's Affirmation _____

Day: _____ *Date:* ____/____/____

Today I am *Grateful* for _____

_____

_____

_____

_____

Today's Affirmation _____

> Happiness resides not in possessions, and not in gold, happiness dwells in the soul. ~ *Democritus*

Day: _____ *Date:* ____/____/____

Today I am *Grateful* for _____

_____

_____

_____

_____

Today's Affirmation _____

Day: _____ *Date:* ____/____/____

Today I am *Grateful* for _____

_____

_____

_____

_____

Today's Affirmation _____

The essence of all beautiful art, all great art, is gratitude.
~ Friedrich Nietzsche

Day: _____ *Date:* ____/____/____

Today I am *Grateful* for _____

_____

_____

_____

_____

Today's Affirmation _____

Day: _____ Date: ____/____/____

Today I am *Grateful* for _____

_____
_____
_____
_____

Today's Affirmation _____

A single grateful thought toward heaven is the most perfect prayer.
~ Gotthold Ephraim Lessing

Day: _____ Date: ____/____/____

Today I am *Grateful* for _____

_____
_____
_____
_____

Today's Affirmation _____

Day: _____ Date: ___/___/___

Today I am *Grateful* for _____

_____
_____
_____
_____

Today's Affirmation _____

The way to know life is to love many things. ~ Vincent Van Gogh

Day: _____ Date: ___/___/___

Today I am *Grateful* for _____

_____
_____
_____
_____

Today's Affirmation _____

Day: _____ *Date:* ____ / ____ / ____

Today I am *Grateful* for _____

_____
_____
_____
_____

Today's Affirmation _____

Gratitude is not only the greatest of virtues, but the parent of all the others.
~ Marcus Tullius Cicero

Day: _____ *Date:* ____ / ____ / ____

Today I am *Grateful* for _____

_____
_____
_____
_____

Today's Affirmation _____

Day: _____ Date: ___/___/___

Today I am *Grateful* for _____

_____
_____
_____
_____

Today's Affirmation _____

Gratitude is the sign of noble souls. ~ *Aesop Fables*

Day: _____ Date: ___/___/___

Today I am *Grateful* for _____

_____
_____
_____
_____

Today's Affirmation _____

Day: _____ *Date:* ____ / ____ / ____

Today I am *Grateful* for _____

_____
_____
_____
_____

Today's Affirmation _____

There is only one way to happiness and that is to cease worrying about things which are beyond the power of our will. ~ *Epictetus*

Day: _____ *Date:* ____ / ____ / ____

Today I am *Grateful* for _____

_____
_____
_____
_____

Today's Affirmation _____

Day: _____ Date: ____/____/____

Today I am *Grateful* for _____
_____
_____
_____
_____

Today's Affirmation _____

Everything has beauty, but not everyone sees it. ~ *Confucius*

Day: _____ Date: ____/____/____

Today I am *Grateful* for _____
_____
_____
_____
_____

Today's Affirmation _____

Day: _____ Date: ____/____/____

Today I am *Grateful* for _____

_____
_____
_____
_____

Today's Affirmation _____

This world is but a canvas to our imagination. ~ Henry David Thoreau

Day: _____ Date: ____/____/____

Today I am *Grateful* for _____

_____
_____
_____
_____

Today's Affirmation _____

Day: _____ *Date:* ____/____/____

Today I am *Grateful* for _____

_____
_____
_____
_____

Today's Affirmation _____

> Real happiness is cheap enough, yet how dearly we pay for its counterfeit.
> ~ *Hosea Ballou*

Day: _____ *Date:* ____/____/____

Today I am *Grateful* for _____

_____
_____
_____
_____

Today's Affirmation _____

Day: _____ *Date:* ____/____/____

Today I am *Grateful* for _____

_____

_____

_____

_____

Today's Affirmation _____

> Never give up, for that is just the place and time that the tide will turn.
> ~ *Harriet Beecher Stowe*

Day: _____ *Date:* ____/____/____

Today I am *Grateful* for _____

_____

_____

_____

_____

Today's Affirmation _____

Day: _____ Date: _____ / _____ / _____

Today I am *Grateful* for _____

_____
_____
_____
_____

Today's Affirmation _____

The power of imagination makes us infinite. ~ John Muir

Day: _____ Date: _____ / _____ / _____

Today I am *Grateful* for _____

_____
_____
_____
_____

Today's Affirmation _____

Day: _____ Date: _____/_____/_____

Today I am *Grateful* for _____

_____

_____

_____

_____

Today's Affirmation _____

Happiness is a choice that requires effort at times. ~ Aeschylus

Day: _____ Date: _____/_____/_____

Today I am *Grateful* for _____

_____

_____

_____

_____

Today's Affirmation _____

Day: _____ Date: ___/___/___

Today I am *Grateful* for _____

_____
_____
_____
_____

Today's Affirmation _____

A contented mind is the greatest blessing a man can enjoy in this world.
~ *Joseph Addison*

Day: _____ Date: ___/___/___

Today I am *Grateful* for _____

_____
_____
_____
_____

Today's Affirmation _____

Day: _____ *Date:* ____/____/____

Today I am *Grateful* for _____

Today's Affirmation _____

What we obtain too cheap, we esteem too lightly; it is dearness only that gives everything its value. ~ *Thomas Paine*

Day: _____ *Date:* ____/____/____

Today I am *Grateful* for _____

Today's Affirmation _____

Day: _____ Date: ___/___/___

Today I am *Grateful* for _____

_____
_____
_____
_____

Today's Affirmation _____

Life in abundance comes only through great love. ~ *Elbert Hubbard*

Day: _____ Date: ___/___/___

Today I am *Grateful* for _____

_____
_____
_____
_____

Today's Affirmation _____

Day: _____ *Date:* ____/____/____

Today I am *Grateful* for _____

_____

_____

_____

_____

Today's Affirmation _____

A loving heart is the beginning of all knowledge. ~ *Thomas Carlyle*

Day: _____ *Date:* ____/____/____

Today I am *Grateful* for _____

_____

_____

_____

_____

Today's Affirmation _____

Day: _____ *Date:* ___/___/___

Today I am *Grateful* for _____

_____
_____
_____
_____

Today's Affirmation _____

> There are two ways of spreading light: to be the candle or the mirror that reflects it. ~ *Edith Wharton*

Day: _____ *Date:* ___/___/___

Today I am *Grateful* for _____

_____
_____
_____
_____

Today's Affirmation _____

Day: _____ Date: ____/____/____

Today I am *Grateful* for _____

_____
_____
_____
_____

Today's Affirmation _____

> How very little can be done under the spirit of fear.
> ~ *Florence Nightingale*

Day: _____ Date: ____/____/____

Today I am *Grateful* for _____

_____
_____
_____
_____

Today's Affirmation _____

Day: _____ Date: ___/___/___

Today I am *Grateful* for _____

_____
_____
_____
_____
_____

Today's Affirmation _____

> Life is not a matter of holding good cards, but of playing a poor hand well.
> ~ *Robert Louis Stevenson*

Day: _____ Date: ___/___/___

Today I am *Grateful* for _____

_____
_____
_____
_____
_____

Today's Affirmation _____

Day: _____ *Date:* ___/___/___

Today I am *Grateful* for _____

_____
_____
_____
_____

Today's Affirmation _____

Who knows, the mind has the key to all things besides.
~ *Amos Bronson Alcott*

Day: _____ *Date:* ___/___/___

Today I am *Grateful* for _____

_____
_____
_____
_____

Today's Affirmation _____

Day: _____ *Date:* ____/____/____

Today I am *Grateful* for _____

_____
_____
_____
_____
_____

Today's Affirmation _____

The purpose creates the machine. ~ *Arthur Young*

Day: _____ *Date:* ____/____/____

Today I am *Grateful* for _____

_____
_____
_____
_____
_____

Today's Affirmation _____

Day: _____ *Date:* ___/___/___

Today I am *Grateful* for _____

_____
_____
_____
_____

Today's Affirmation _____

> Knowing is not enough; we must apply. Willing is not enough; we must do.
> ~ *Johann Wolfgang von Goethe*

Day: _____ *Date:* ___/___/___

Today I am *Grateful* for _____

_____
_____
_____
_____

Today's Affirmation _____

Day: _____ *Date:* ____/____/____

Today I am *Grateful* for _____

_____

_____

_____

_____

Today's Affirmation _____

> True originality consists not in a new manner but in a new vision.
> ~ *Edith Wharton*

Day: _____ *Date:* ____/____/____

Today I am *Grateful* for _____

_____

_____

_____

_____

Today's Affirmation _____

Day: _____ *Date:* ____ / ____ / ____

Today I am *Grateful* for _____

_____

_____

_____

_____

Today's Affirmation _____

What is once well done is done forever.
~ *Henry David Thoreau*

Day: _____ *Date:* ____ / ____ / ____

Today I am *Grateful* for _____

_____

_____

_____

_____

Today's Affirmation _____

Day: _____ Date: ___/___/___

Today I am *Grateful* for _____

_____
_____
_____
_____

Today's Affirmation _____

> Live your life as though your every act were to become a universal law.
> ~ *Immanuel Kant*

Day: _____ Date: ___/___/___

Today I am *Grateful* for _____

_____
_____
_____
_____

Today's Affirmation _____

Day: _____ Date: ____/____/____

Today I am *Grateful* for _____

_____
_____
_____
_____

Today's Affirmation _____

If you want the present to be different from the past, study the past.
~ Baruch Spinoza

Day: _____ Date: ____/____/____

Today I am *Grateful* for _____

_____
_____
_____
_____

Today's Affirmation _____

Day: _____ Date: ____/____/____

Today I am *Grateful* for _____

_____
_____
_____
_____

Today's Affirmation _____

> The best preparation for tomorrow is to do today's work superbly well.
> ~ *William Osler*

Day: _____ Date: ____/____/____

Today I am *Grateful* for _____

_____
_____
_____
_____

Today's Affirmation _____

Day: _____ *Date:* ____/____/____

Today I am *Grateful* for _____

_____
_____
_____
_____

Today's Affirmation _____

Remember when life's path is steep to keep your mind even. ~ *Horace*

Day: _____ *Date:* ____/____/____

Today I am *Grateful* for _____

_____
_____
_____
_____

Today's Affirmation _____

Day: _____ *Date:* ____/____/____

Today I am *Grateful* for _____

_____
_____
_____
_____

Today's Affirmation _____

Ask me not what I have, but what I am. ~ *Heinrich Heine*

Day: _____ *Date:* ____/____/____

Today I am *Grateful* for _____

_____
_____
_____
_____

Today's Affirmation _____

Day: _____ *Date:* ___/___/___

Today I am *Grateful* for _____

_____
_____
_____
_____

Today's Affirmation _____

> Great thoughts speak only to the thoughtful mind, but great actions speak to all mankind. ~ *Theodore Roosevelt*

Day: _____ *Date:* ___/___/___

Today I am *Grateful* for _____

_____
_____
_____
_____

Today's Affirmation _____

Day: _____ Date: ___/___/___

Today I am *Grateful* for _____

_____
_____
_____
_____

Today's Affirmation _____

> To love oneself is the beginning of a lifelong romance.
> ~ *Oscar Wilde*

Day: _____ Date: ___/___/___

Today I am *Grateful* for _____

_____
_____
_____
_____

Today's Affirmation _____

Day: _____ *Date:* ___/___/___

Today I am *Grateful* for _____

_____
_____
_____
_____

Today's Affirmation _____

> It is our attitude at the beginning of a difficult task which, more than anything else, will affect its successful outcome. ~ *William James*

Day: _____ *Date:* ___/___/___

Today I am *Grateful* for _____

_____
_____
_____
_____

Today's Affirmation _____

Day: _____ Date: ___/___/___

Today I am *Grateful* for _____

_____
_____
_____
_____

Today's Affirmation _____

Cheerfulness is the best promoter of health and is as friendly to the mind as to the body. ~ Joseph Addison

Day: _____ Date: ___/___/___

Today I am *Grateful* for _____

_____
_____
_____
_____

Today's Affirmation _____

Day: _____ Date: ____/____/____

Today I am *Grateful* for _____

_____
_____
_____
_____

Today's Affirmation _____

It is costly wisdom that is bought by experience. ~ *Roger Ascham*

Day: _____ Date: ____/____/____

Today I am *Grateful* for _____

_____
_____
_____
_____

Today's Affirmation _____

Day: _____ *Date:* ____/____/____

Today I am *Grateful* for _____

_____
_____
_____
_____

Today's Affirmation _____

Love always brings difficulties, that is true, but the good side of it is that it gives energy. ~ *Vincent Van Gogh*

Day: _____ *Date:* ____/____/____

Today I am *Grateful* for _____

_____
_____
_____
_____

Today's Affirmation _____

Day: _____ *Date:* ____/____/____

Today I am *Grateful* for _____

_____

_____

_____

_____

Today's Affirmation _____

> A thousand words will not leave so deep an impression as one deed.
> ~ *Henrik Ibsen*

Day: _____ *Date:* ____/____/____

Today I am *Grateful* for _____

_____

_____

_____

_____

Today's Affirmation _____

Day: _____ Date: ___/___/___

Today I am *Grateful* for _____

_____
_____
_____
_____

Today's Affirmation _____

> All experience is an arch, to build upon.
> ~ *Henry Adams*

Day: _____ Date: ___/___/___

Today I am *Grateful* for _____

_____
_____
_____
_____

Today's Affirmation _____

Day: _____ Date: ____/____/____

Today I am *Grateful* for _____

_____
_____
_____
_____

Today's Affirmation _____

> A thing of beauty is a joy forever: its loveliness increases; it will never pass into nothingness. ~ *John Keats*

Day: _____ Date: ____/____/____

Today I am *Grateful* for _____

_____
_____
_____
_____

Today's Affirmation _____

Day: _____ Date: ___/___/___

Today I am *Grateful* for _____
_____
_____
_____
_____

Today's Affirmation _____

To have courage for whatever comes in life - everything lies in that.
~ Saint Teresa of Avila

Day: _____ Date: ___/___/___

Today I am *Grateful* for _____
_____
_____
_____
_____

Today's Affirmation _____

Day: _____ Date: ____/____/____

Today I am *Grateful* for _____

_____
_____
_____
_____

Today's Affirmation _____

Thank God every morning when you get up that you have something to do that day, which must be done, whether you like it or not. ~ *James Russell Lowell*

Day: _____ Date: ____/____/____

Today I am *Grateful* for _____

_____
_____
_____
_____

Today's Affirmation _____

Day: _____ Date: ___/___/___

Today I am *Grateful* for _____

_____
_____
_____
_____

Today's Affirmation _____

> Gratitude is a duty which ought to be paid, but which none have a right to expect. ~ *Jean-Jacques Rousseau*

Day: _____ Date: ___/___/___

Today I am *Grateful* for _____

_____
_____
_____
_____

Today's Affirmation _____

Day: _____ Date: ____/____/____

Today I am *Grateful* for _____

_____
_____
_____
_____

Today's Affirmation _____

> Little minds are interested in the extraordinary; great minds in the commonplace. ~ *Elbert Hubbard*

Day: _____ Date: ____/____/____

Today I am *Grateful* for _____

_____
_____
_____
_____

Today's Affirmation _____

Day: _____ Date: ____/____/____

Today I am *Grateful* for _____

_____
_____
_____
_____

Today's Affirmation _____

> When you're finished changing, you're finished.
> ~ Benjamin Franklin

Day: _____ Date: ____/____/____

Today I am *Grateful* for _____

_____
_____
_____
_____

Today's Affirmation _____

Day: _____ Date: ____/____/____

Today I am *Grateful* for _____

_____
_____
_____
_____
_____

Today's Affirmation _____

Appreciation is a wonderful thing: It makes what is excellent in others belong to us as well. ~ Voltaire

Day: _____ Date: ____/____/____

Today I am *Grateful* for _____

_____
_____
_____
_____
_____

Today's Affirmation _____

Day: _____ Date: ___/___/___

Today I am *Grateful* for _____

_____
_____
_____
_____

Today's Affirmation _____

> Creativity is not the finding of a thing, but the making something out of it after it is found. ~ *James Russell Lowell*

Day: _____ Date: ___/___/___

Today I am *Grateful* for _____

_____
_____
_____
_____

Today's Affirmation _____

Day: _____ Date: ____/____/____

Today I am *Grateful* for _____

_____
_____
_____
_____
_____

Today's Affirmation _____

> With an eye made quiet by the power of harmony, and the deep power of joy, we see into the life of things. ~ *William Wordsworth*

Day: _____ Date: ____/____/____

Today I am *Grateful* for _____

_____
_____
_____
_____
_____

Today's Affirmation _____

Day: _____ Date: ____/____/____

Today I am *Grateful* for _____

_____
_____
_____
_____

Today's Affirmation _____

> We consume our tomorrows fretting about our yesterdays. ~ *Persius*

Day: _____ Date: ____/____/____

Today I am *Grateful* for _____

_____
_____
_____
_____

Today's Affirmation _____

Day: _____ Date: ____/____/____

Today I am *Grateful* for _____

_____
_____
_____
_____

Today's Affirmation _____

> You cannot do a kindness too soon, for you never know how soon it will be too late. ~ *Ralph Waldo Emerson*

Day: _____ Date: ____/____/____

Today I am *Grateful* for _____

_____
_____
_____
_____

Today's Affirmation _____

Day: _____ *Date:* ___/___/___

Today I am *Grateful* for _____

_____
_____
_____
_____

Today's Affirmation _____

> Genius is the ability to renew one's emotions in daily experience.
> ~ *Paul Cezanne*

Day: _____ *Date:* ___/___/___

Today I am *Grateful* for _____

_____
_____
_____
_____

Today's Affirmation _____

Day: _____ *Date:* ____/____/____

Today I am *Grateful* for _____

_____

_____

_____

_____

Today's Affirmation _____

> The measure of a man's real character is what he would do if he knew he would never be found out. ~ *Thomas Babington Macaulay*

Day: _____ *Date:* ____/____/____

Today I am *Grateful* for _____

_____

_____

_____

_____

Today's Affirmation _____

Day: _____ *Date:* ___/___/___

Today I am *Grateful* for _____

_____

_____

_____

_____

Today's Affirmation _____

Begin, be bold and venture to be wise. ~ *Horace*

Day: _____ *Date:* ___/___/___

Today I am *Grateful* for _____

_____

_____

_____

_____

Today's Affirmation _____

Day: _____ Date: ____/____/____

Today I am *Grateful* for _____

_____
_____
_____
_____

Today's Affirmation _____

> I dwell in possibility.
> ~ *Emily Dickinson*

Day: _____ Date: ____/____/____

Today I am *Grateful* for _____

_____
_____
_____
_____

Today's Affirmation _____

Day: _____ *Date:* ___/___/___

Today I am *Grateful* for _____

_____
_____
_____
_____

Today's Affirmation _____

If we learn not humility, we learn nothing. ~ *John Jewel*

Day: _____ *Date:* ___/___/___

Today I am *Grateful* for _____

_____
_____
_____
_____

Today's Affirmation _____

Day: _____ *Date:* ____ / ____ / ____

Today I am *Grateful* for _____

_____

_____

_____

_____

Today's Affirmation _____

If there is no struggle, there is no progress.
~ *Frederick Douglass*

Day: _____ *Date:* ____ / ____ / ____

Today I am *Grateful* for _____

_____

_____

_____

_____

Today's Affirmation _____

Day: _____ Date: ___/___/___

Today I am *Grateful* for _____

_____
_____
_____
_____

Today's Affirmation _____

> The art of being wise is the art of knowing what to overlook.
> ~ *William James*

Day: _____ Date: ___/___/___

Today I am *Grateful* for _____

_____
_____
_____
_____

Today's Affirmation _____

Day: _____ *Date:* ____/____/____

Today I am *Grateful* for _____

_____
_____
_____
_____

Today's Affirmation _____

Let the beauty of what you love be what you do. ~ *Rumi*

Day: _____ *Date:* ____/____/____

Today I am *Grateful* for _____

_____
_____
_____
_____

Today's Affirmation _____

Day: _____ *Date:* ___/___/___

Today I am *Grateful* for _____

_____
_____
_____
_____

Today's Affirmation _____

> When I let go of what I am, I become what I might be.
> ~ *Lao Tzu*

Day: _____ *Date:* ___/___/___

Today I am *Grateful* for _____

_____
_____
_____
_____

Today's Affirmation _____

Day: _____ *Date:* ____/____/____

Today I am *Grateful* for _____

_____
_____
_____
_____

Today's Affirmation _____

> Seek not to understand that you may believe, but believe that you may understand. ~ *Saint Augustine*

Day: _____ *Date:* ____/____/____

Today I am *Grateful* for _____

_____
_____
_____
_____

Today's Affirmation _____

Day: _____ Date: ___/___/___

Today I am *Grateful* for _____

_____
_____
_____
_____

Today's Affirmation _____

Our life is what our thoughts make it. ~ Marcus Aurelius

Day: _____ Date: ___/___/___

Today I am *Grateful* for _____

_____
_____
_____
_____

Today's Affirmation _____

Day: _____ Date: ____/____/____

Today I am *Grateful* for _____

_____
_____
_____
_____

Today's Affirmation _____

They succeed, because they think they can. ~ *Virgil*

Day: _____ Date: ____/____/____

Today I am *Grateful* for _____

_____
_____
_____
_____

Today's Affirmation _____

Day: _____ Date: ___/___/___

Today I am *Grateful* for _____

_____
_____
_____
_____

Today's Affirmation _____

> Success consists of getting up just one more time than you fall.
> ~ *Oliver Goldsmith*

Day: _____ Date: ___/___/___

Today I am *Grateful* for _____

_____
_____
_____
_____

Today's Affirmation _____

Day: _____ Date: ____/____/____

Today I am *Grateful* for _____

_____
_____
_____
_____

Today's Affirmation _____

Nothing would be done at all if one waited until one could do it so well that no one could find fault with it. ~ John Henry Newman

Day: _____ Date: ____/____/____

Today I am *Grateful* for _____

_____
_____
_____
_____

Today's Affirmation _____

Day: _____ Date: ___/___/___

Today I am *Grateful* for _____

_____
_____
_____
_____

Today's Affirmation _____

Good actions give strength to ourselves and inspire good actions in others.
~ Plato

Day: _____ Date: ___/___/___

Today I am *Grateful* for _____

_____
_____
_____
_____

Today's Affirmation _____

Day: _____ *Date:* ____ / ____ / ____

Today I am *Grateful* for _____

_____

_____

_____

_____

Today's Affirmation _____

Life consists not in holding good cards but in playing those you hold well.
~ *Josh Billings*

Day: _____ *Date:* ____ / ____ / ____

Today I am *Grateful* for _____

_____

_____

_____

_____

Today's Affirmation _____

Day: _____ *Date:* ___/___/___

Today I am *Grateful* for _____

_____
_____
_____
_____

Today's Affirmation _____

Do not take life too seriously. You will never get out of it alive.
~ *Elbert Hubbard*

Day: _____ *Date:* ___/___/___

Today I am *Grateful* for _____

_____
_____
_____
_____

Today's Affirmation _____

Day: _____ Date: ____/____/____

Today I am *Grateful* for _____

_____
_____
_____
_____

Today's Affirmation _____

When unhappy, one doubts everything; when happy, one doubts nothing.
~ Joseph Roux

Day: _____ Date: ____/____/____

Today I am *Grateful* for _____

_____
_____
_____
_____

Today's Affirmation _____

Day: _____ *Date:* ____/____/____

Today I am *Grateful* for _____

_____

_____

_____

_____

Today's Affirmation _____

> The things that we love tell us what we are. ~ *Thomas Aquinas*

Day: _____ *Date:* ____/____/____

Today I am *Grateful* for _____

_____

_____

_____

_____

Today's Affirmation _____

Day: _____ *Date:* ___/___/___

Today I am *Grateful* for _____

_____
_____
_____
_____

Today's Affirmation _____

> No man is an island, entire of itself; every man is a piece of the continent.
> ~ - *John Donne*

Day: _____ *Date:* ___/___/___

Today I am *Grateful* for _____

_____
_____
_____
_____

Today's Affirmation _____

Day: _____ Date: ___/___/___

Today I am *Grateful* for _____

_____
_____
_____
_____

Today's Affirmation _____

Friends are the sunshine of life. ~ *John Hay*

Day: _____ Date: ___/___/___

Today I am *Grateful* for _____

_____
_____
_____
_____

Today's Affirmation _____

Day: _____ Date: ____/____/____

Today I am *Grateful* for _____

_____
_____
_____
_____

Today's Affirmation _____

There is nothing like a dream to create the future. ~ *Victor Hugo*

Day: _____ Date: ____/____/____

Today I am *Grateful* for _____

_____
_____
_____
_____

Today's Affirmation _____

Day: _____ Date: ___/___/___

Today I am *Grateful* for _____

_____
_____
_____
_____

Today's Affirmation _____

> The strongest principle of growth lies in the human choice.
> ~ *George Eliot*

Day: _____ Date: ___/___/___

Today I am *Grateful* for _____

_____
_____
_____
_____

Today's Affirmation _____

Day: _____ *Date:* ____/____/____

Today I am *Grateful* for _____

_____
_____
_____
_____
_____

Today's Affirmation _____

Absence sharpens love, presence strengthens it. ~ *Thomas Fuller*

Day: _____ *Date:* ____/____/____

Today I am *Grateful* for _____

_____
_____
_____
_____
_____

Today's Affirmation _____

Day: _____ *Date:* ___/___/___

Today I am *Grateful* for _____

_____
_____
_____
_____

Today's Affirmation _____

What worries you, masters you. ~ *John Locke*

Day: _____ *Date:* ___/___/___

Today I am *Grateful* for _____

_____
_____
_____
_____

Today's Affirmation _____

Day: _____ *Date:* ____/____/____

Today I am *Grateful* for _____

_____

_____

_____

_____

Today's Affirmation _____

> Events will take their course, it is no good of being angry at them; he is happiest who wisely turns them to the best account. ~ *Euripides*

Day: _____ *Date:* ____/____/____

Today I am *Grateful* for _____

_____

_____

_____

_____

Today's Affirmation _____

Day: _____ Date: ___/___/___

Today I am *Grateful* for _____

_____
_____
_____
_____

Today's Affirmation _____

Truly, it is in darkness that one finds the light, so when we are in sorrow, then this light is nearest of all to us. ~ Meister Eckhart

Day: _____ Date: ___/___/___

Today I am *Grateful* for _____

_____
_____
_____
_____

Today's Affirmation _____

Day: _____ Date: ____/____/____

Today I am *Grateful* for _____

_____
_____
_____
_____
_____

Today's Affirmation _____

> Nothing will ever be attempted if all possible objections must first be overcome. ~ *Samuel Johnson*

Day: _____ Date: ____/____/____

Today I am *Grateful* for _____

_____
_____
_____
_____
_____

Today's Affirmation _____

Day: _____ Date: ____/____/____

Today I am *Grateful* for _____

_____
_____
_____
_____

Today's Affirmation _____

> You must accept the truth from whatever source it comes.
> ~ *Maimonides*

Day: _____ Date: ____/____/____

Today I am *Grateful* for _____

_____
_____
_____
_____

Today's Affirmation _____

Day: _____ *Date:* ____/____/____

Today I am *Grateful* for _____

_____
_____
_____
_____

Today's Affirmation _____

Our opportunities to do good are our talents. ~ *Cotton Mather*

Day: _____ *Date:* ____/____/____

Today I am *Grateful* for _____

_____
_____
_____
_____

Today's Affirmation _____

Day: _____ Date: ___/___/___

Today I am *Grateful* for _____

_____
_____
_____
_____

Today's Affirmation _____

Either I will find a way, or I will make one. ~ *Philip Sidney*

Day: _____ Date: ___/___/___

Today I am *Grateful* for _____

_____
_____
_____
_____

Today's Affirmation _____

Day: _____ Date: ____/____/____

Today I am *Grateful* for _____

_____
_____
_____
_____
_____

Today's Affirmation _____

> We love life, not because we are used to living but because we are used to loving. ~ *Friedrich Nietzsche*

Day: _____ Date: ____/____/____

Today I am *Grateful* for _____

_____
_____
_____
_____
_____

Today's Affirmation _____

Day: _____ Date: ___/___/___

Today I am *Grateful* for _____

_____
_____
_____
_____

Today's Affirmation _____

If you wished to be loved, love. ~ *Lucius Annaeus Seneca*

Day: _____ Date: ___/___/___

Today I am *Grateful* for _____

_____
_____
_____
_____

Today's Affirmation _____

Day: _____ Date: ___/___/___

Today I am *Grateful* for _____

_____
_____
_____
_____
_____

Today's Affirmation _____

It does not matter how slowly you go as long as you do not stop.
~ *Confucius*

Day: _____ Date: ___/___/___

Today I am *Grateful* for _____

_____
_____
_____
_____
_____

Today's Affirmation _____

Day: _____ *Date:* ___/___/___

Today I am *Grateful* for _____

_____
_____
_____
_____

Today's Affirmation _____

> Love has reasons which reason cannot understand.
> ~ *Blaise Pascal*

Day: _____ *Date:* ___/___/___

Today I am *Grateful* for _____

_____
_____
_____
_____

Today's Affirmation _____

Day: _____ Date: ____/____/____

Today I am *Grateful* for _____

_____
_____
_____
_____
_____

Today's Affirmation _____

> We are here to add what we can to life, not to get what we can from life.
> ~ *William Osler*

Day: _____ Date: ____/____/____

Today I am *Grateful* for _____

_____
_____
_____
_____
_____

Today's Affirmation _____

Day: _____ Date: ___/___/___

Today I am *Grateful* for _____
_____
_____
_____
_____

Today's Affirmation _____

True knowledge exists in knowing that you know nothing. ~ *Socrates*

Day: _____ Date: ___/___/___

Today I am *Grateful* for _____
_____
_____
_____
_____

Today's Affirmation _____

Day: _____ *Date:* ____/____/____

Today I am *Grateful* for _____

_____
_____
_____
_____

Today's Affirmation _____

It's not what happens to you, but how you react to it that matters.
~ *Epictetus*

Day: _____ *Date:* ____/____/____

Today I am *Grateful* for _____

_____
_____
_____
_____

Today's Affirmation _____

Day: _____ *Date:* ___/___/___

Today I am *Grateful* for _____

_____

_____

_____

_____

Today's Affirmation _____

Fortune favors the bold. ~ *Virgil*

Day: _____ *Date:* ___/___/___

Today I am *Grateful* for _____

_____

_____

_____

_____

Today's Affirmation _____

Day: _____ Date: ____/____/____

Today I am *Grateful* for _____

_____
_____
_____
_____
_____

Today's Affirmation _____

> That which does not kill us makes us stronger.
> ~ Friedrich Nietzsche

Day: _____ Date: ____/____/____

Today I am *Grateful* for _____

_____
_____
_____
_____
_____

Today's Affirmation _____

Day: _____ *Date:* ___/___/___

Today I am *Grateful* for _____

_____
_____
_____
_____

Today's Affirmation _____

> As people are walking all the time, in the same spot, a path appears.
> ~ John Locke

Day: _____ *Date:* ___/___/___

Today I am *Grateful* for _____

_____
_____
_____
_____

Today's Affirmation _____

Manufactured by Amazon.ca
Acheson, AB